BEEHIVES

Nature's Engineers

Christopher Forest

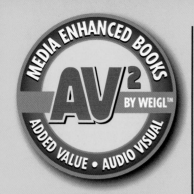

AV² provides enriched content that supplements and complements this book. Weigl's AV² books strive to create inspired learning and engage young minds in a total learning experience.

Your AV² Media Enhanced books come alive with...

Audio
Listen to sections of the book read aloud.

Video
Watch informative video clips.

Embedded Weblinks
Gain additional information for research.

Try This!
Complete activities and hands-on experiments.

Key Words
Study vocabulary, and complete a matching word activity.

Quizzes
Test your knowledge.

Slide Show
View images and captions, and prepare a presentation.

... and much, much more!

Go to **www.av2books.com**, and enter this book's unique code.

BOOK CODE

AVN38938

AV² by Weigl brings you media enhanced books that support active learning.

Published by AV² by Weigl
350 5th Avenue, 59th Floor
New York, NY 10118
Website: www.av2books.com

Library of Congress Cataloging-in-Publication Data

Names: Forest, Christopher, author.
Title: Beehives / Christopher Forest.
Description: New York, NY : AV2 by Weigl, [2019] | Series: Nature's engineers | Audience: K to Grade 3. | Includes bibliographical references and index.
Identifiers: LCCN 2018053405 (print) | LCCN 2018054182 (ebook) | ISBN 9781489697479 (Multi User ebook) | ISBN 9781489697486 (Single User ebook) | ISBN 9781489697455 (hardcover : alk. paper) | ISBN 9781489697462 (softcover : alk. paper)
Subjects: LCSH: Beehives--Juvenile literature.
Classification: LCC SF532 (ebook) | LCC SF532 .F67 2019 (print) | DDC 638/.14--dc23
LC record available at https://lccn.loc.gov/2018053405

Printed in Guangzhou, China
1 2 3 4 5 6 7 8 9 0 23 2 22 21 20 19
·
012019
102318

Project Coordinator: Heather Kissock
Art Director: Terry Paulhus

Photo Credits
Every reasonable effort has been made to trace ownership and to obtain permission to reprint copyright material. The publishers would be pleased to have any errors or omissions brought to their attention so that they may be corrected in subsequent printings.

Weigl acknowledges Getty Images, Alamy, iStock, and Shutterstock as its primary image suppliers for this title.

First published by North Star Editions in 2019.

BEEHIVES
Nature's Engineers

CONTENTS

CHAPTER 1

BUSY AS A BEE

A **swarm** of bees flies to an oak tree. The bees gather around a large hole in the trunk. One bee enters the hole. The others follow. They fly to a nest deep inside the tree. This nest is called a beehive.

FUN FACT

Bees that live together in hives are known as social bees.

A bee **colony** lives inside the hive. There are three kinds of bees in a colony. They work together. Each kind of bee has a different job.

The **queen** bee lays eggs. When the eggs hatch, worker bees feed and protect the **larvae**. Workers also build and repair the hive. One colony usually has thousands of workers.

All worker bees are female. Male bees are called drones. They **mate** with the queen.

WORKING TOGETHER

Each hive has only one queen bee. A hive also includes a few hundred drones. But most bees in a hive are workers. A typical hive can be home to 35,000 bees during the summer. That number drops down to approximately 5,000 bees in the winter.

FUN FACT

In summer, worker bees live for approximately one month. In winter, workers can live for several months. This is because there is less to do.

Every spring, bee colonies split. One-third of the colony stays in the hive. The rest of the bees leave. They go build a new hive.

A group of workers, called scouts, searches for the perfect spot. They look for a cave, rock, branch, or hollow tree. Then, the scouts report their findings to the other bees. Scouts try to convince other bees to choose their site. To do so, they wiggle their bodies.

Once the bees choose a site, they build the hive. A hive is made from light-colored wax. The worker bees **secrete** the wax. Their bodies turn sugar from honey into wax. The wax leaves their bodies through their **pores**.

Workers shape the wax into cells. Some bees chew on the wax to help shape it. Each cell has six sides. A group of cells is called a comb.

FUN FACT

Worker bees collect a substance called propolis from trees. They use it as glue to repair the hive.

THE PERFECT SHAPE

The six sides of a beehive cell form a hexagon. Bees use this shape for many reasons. Hexagons have straight edges. They fit together well. As a result, bees can form combs with no gaps between cells. This makes it easy to add new combs to the hive.

Grouping cells together makes more space for storage. The hexagon shape also lessens the wall space between cells. This allows bees to use less wax. The wax is easy to bend. But the hexagon shape makes the cells strong.

INSIDE THE HIVE

A hive has several types of cells. Some cells hold eggs or larvae. Others hold food. One type is the storage cell. Storage cells are in the upper part of a comb. Bees use them to hold **nectar** and **pollen**.

FUN FACT

Each cell that holds a bee larva is less than 0.4 inches (10 millimeters) wide.

Bees leave the hive to collect pollen and nectar. They fly from flower to flower. They take pollen and nectar from each one. Then, they return to the hive.

Some bees, such as honeybees, turn nectar into honey. They store the honey in their comb.

Another type of cell is the drone cell. Drone cells hold larvae. The larvae grow to become male bees. Drone cells are in the lower part of a comb.

Worker cells also hold larvae. But they are smaller than drone cells. The larvae in these cells become worker bees.

Sometimes, bees make queen cells. These long, tall cells hang down from the comb. The queen lays eggs inside them. When the eggs hatch, workers feed the larvae **royal jelly**. All bee larvae eat royal jelly. But most eat pollen and nectar, too. If a larva eats only royal jelly, it will become a queen.

FUN FACT

A queen bee can lay more than 2,000 eggs each day.

CHAPTER 4

NATURE'S HELPERS

Beehives have a major impact on the **habitat** around them. When bees gather pollen, they spread it from plant to plant. This process is called pollination. Plants need pollen to create fruit and seeds.

Without bees to spread pollen, many plants cannot make seeds. Flowers and trees could die. Many fruits and vegetables depend on bees, too. If there are no bees, they cannot grow. People and animals might not have food to eat.

A hive's honey and wax also help other animals. Animals such as honey badgers and bears eat honey. Some animals even eat beeswax.

FUN FACT

In one year, a bee colony can make up to 100 pounds (45 kilograms) of honey.

Beehives also benefit humans. Humans eat honey. They use it to sweeten their food. Some people even build artificial hives for bees to live in. The bees make combs and honey inside. Beekeepers care for the bees and collect their honey.

Humans also use the wax from hives. Beeswax is used to make a variety of items. It is in candles, beauty products, and medicines.

Each hive is built to protect and feed a bee colony. But it helps many other plants and animals. And the hive's amazing structure helps make all this possible.

THE BEEHIVES QUIZ

1 What is a bee's home known as?

2 How many kinds of bees live inside a colony?

4 What kind of worker bees search for new spots to build a hive?

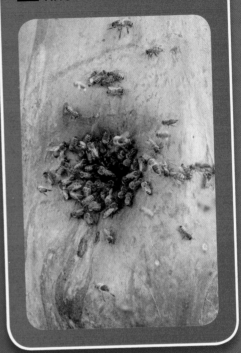

3 What do worker bees secrete to build the hive?

5 What is the shape of a beehive cell?

6 Where in the hive do bees store nectar and pollen?

7 To become a queen, what must a larva eat instead of pollen and nectar?

8 What are people who care for bees and collect their honey called?

KEY WORDS

colony: a group of animals that live together

habitat: the type of place where plants or animals normally grow or live

larvae: insects that have hatched from eggs and are in the early stages of life

mate: joins together in order to have babies

nectar: a sweet liquid released by plants that bees use to make honey

pollen: a fine powder produced by some plants that helps create new plants

pores: tiny holes in the body

queen: a large female bee that lays the eggs for a bee colony

royal jelly: a thick, milky substance that worker bees make using glands in their throats. It is used as food for bee larvae.

secrete: to release something through the skin

swarm: a large number of bees flying together

INDEX

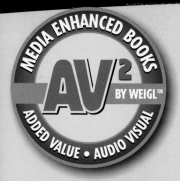

Log on to www.av2books.com

AV[2] by Weigl brings you media enhanced books that support active learning. Go to www.av2books.com, and enter the special code found on page 2 of this book. You will gain access to enriched and enhanced content that supplements and complements this book. Content includes video, audio, weblinks, quizzes, a slide show, and activities.

AV[2] Online Navigation

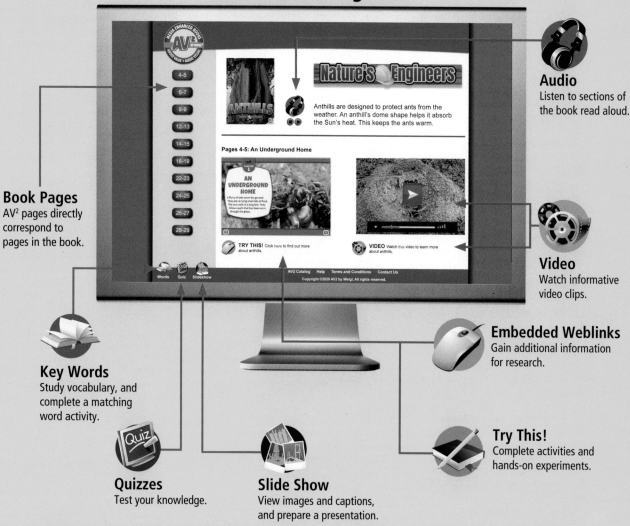

Audio
Listen to sections of the book read aloud.

Book Pages
AV[2] pages directly correspond to pages in the book.

Video
Watch informative video clips.

Key Words
Study vocabulary, and complete a matching word activity.

Embedded Weblinks
Gain additional information for research.

Try This!
Complete activities and hands-on experiments.

Quizzes
Test your knowledge.

Slide Show
View images and captions, and prepare a presentation.

AV[2] was built to bridge the gap between print and digital. We encourage you to tell us what you like and what you want to see in the future.

Sign up to be an AV[2] Ambassador at www.av2books.com/ambassador.